Praise for (

"Cool, time-relevant spells
...emphasizing personal responsibility and empow-
erment. This is the handbook for the new breed of
spiritual warrior—teenagers!"

—Michele Morgan, author of *Simple Wicca*

"This kind-hearted charm book is just the thing to
help a teen (or even pre-teen) through the rocky
shoals of youth, while at the same time introducing
him or her to the true meaning of the religion of
Witchcraft, the Craft of the Wise."

—Dana Kramer-Rolls, author of *The Way of the Cat*

"Charm Spells is the perfect gift for any teenager or
young adult who wants to gain more control over
his or her life. Focusing on what we want in life is
usually half the battle. The other half is putting our
desires into motion and manifesting the life we want
to live."

—Ariana, author of *House Magic: The Good Witch's
Guide to Bringing Grace to Your Space*

charm spells

charm spells

white magic for love and friendship, school and home

Ileana Abrev

CONARI PRESS

First published in 2004 by Conari Press,
an imprint of Red Wheel/Weiser, LLC
York Beach, ME
With offices at:
368 Congress Street
Boston, MA 02210
www.redwheelweiser.com

Library of Congress Cataloging-in-Publication Data
Abrev, Ileana.
  Charm spells : white magic for love and friendship, school and home /
Ileana Abrev.
      p. cm.
  Includes index.
  ISBN 1-57324-959-9 (alk. paper)
  1. Magic. I. Title.
  BF1611.A47 2004
  133.4'3—dc22

                          2004009558

Typeset in BeLucian and Fontesque by Kathleen Wilson Fivel
Illustrations by Béatrice Favreau, Contact Jupiter
Printed in Canada
TCP
11 10 09 08 07 06 05 04
 8 7 6 5 4 3 2 1
The paper used in this publication meets the minimum requirements of
the American National Standard for Information Sciences—Permanence
of Paper for Printed Library Materials Z39.48-1992 (R1997).

Dedication

Beverly, I love you.

Robert, my dear teen friend, may the God and Goddess guide you always.

To Cori, thank you for coming up with great spell names.

To Kylie, thank you from the bottom of my heart.

Contents

chapter one
Introduction to Magic

If you use this book wisely, your dreams are sure to come true because we are all beings of light and members of the universal forces. This membership is free to all and does not discriminate against beings of any color, race, or religious belief or background. To join, you only need a positive attitude, an understanding of right and wrong, and the ability to visualize your unselfish needs to the universe.

This membership provides potential much greater than you've ever known, and once the doors open, the possibilities are endless for you to have and to hold. Unfortunately, your membership could be revoked if you do anything against the laws of *karma*—the universe's justice system that keeps the balance of good and evil—and it may take a few weeks, months, or even years for the "Karma Committee" to let you back in.

This is why you should not use spells just because magic is "in" or "trendy." Magic is not a game or a way to control or manipulate others. If you have this in mind, read on to learn the consequences, and then leave this book behind—you are not mature enough to walk the path and not eligible to join.

Positive thinking and visualization are all you need,

and when you add a little bit of this herb and a little bit of that incense, you can make all the necessary changes in your life. You will only be a teen once in this lifetime, so enjoy the laughter and the tears, and accept them as part of growing up. And while you do, you will learn of the positive and negative sides within you, thereby creating a better understanding of yourself in the years to come.

I once had a young teen approach me and ask what he could do to find the person who stole a few CDs from his best friend's backpack at school—but first he let me know that he didn't believe in any of my "hocus pocus," as he called it. I just laughed and gave him a simple spell that involved using a red candle, sprinkling black pepper around it, and asking the universe to let the person who took the CDs come forth and declare his or her wrongdoings.

Two weeks later, he returned and informed me that he had done the spell and, to his surprise, the person who had stolen the CDs did come forward, bragging and admitting that he was the one who took them. My young friend didn't tell me what transpired, but the CDs were returned to his friend's backpack two days later during lunchtime.

This teen wanted to help his friend so badly that

there was nothing in his way, nothing to stop him from focusing on finding out what he wanted to know. This is why you guys make such great magicians. The words NO and YOU CAN'T are not yet filed in your teen memory format.

We adults always think, "What if?" but with you guys it's, "Why not?"

If you have a particular need, that need becomes an arrow, ready to strike the red juicy apple. You are so focused on your needs that nothing will stop you from hitting the designated target, and under no circumstances will that juicy apple be let out of your sight. I hate to tell you this, but your hormones drive your determination and direction, and once you set your mind on something, you will stop at nothing to get it. We parents know this all too well.

As a rule, always think before you act. Remember that no one can force you to do anything you don't want to do. Be yourself, and if your peers don't like it, then it becomes their problem, not yours. Just remember, insecurities are brought on by low self-esteem and not believing in yourself.

Charm Spells will guide you to understand the universe and its mysteries by having faith in yourself and a positive outlook on life. It will teach you to use natural energies to turn your dreams into reality that will benefit you for the rest of your life.

Before you do any of the spells in *Charm Spells*, I would strongly suggest that you read the following chapters. I know you are just itching to get started, but it is worth the read, as the following information will help you to perform the spells.

A guide and a code to always remember: Say no when someone wants you to go against your own principles, and you will find a new respect within that no one will ever destroy or change, throughout this existence.

Have fun, help others, and harm none,
for this is the code of three, and respect it I will!

Blessed be
Ileana

chapter two
What Are Positive and Negative Magic?

To know magic you must understand the balance of positive and negative, because without it, there is no balance of the soul. People make a big issue of the white and black side of witchcraft, but a witch is just a witch, neither white nor black. We can all choose how we apply our magic, either negatively or positively.

A soul that is pure and sure is a happy soul that could only practice a positive lifestyle, but souls that are filled with hatred and jealousy could only commit negative actions towards themselves and others. This best describes the black and white side of magic, but between you and me, those souls that seek destruction towards others are not true practitioners.

Magic occurs once you set your mind to accomplish a goal in your life—it has nothing to do with "Hocus Pocus." The power of positive thinking and visualization creates magic. If you believe in your actions, yourself, and the universe, your needs are fulfilled in front of your eyes, and when they are, you can only create positive magic.

Not only can we create positive magic, but sadly we can also create negative magic. If you set yourself to think negatively towards others or even yourself, you will send a wave of negative thought patterns to the universe, and in time they will come back the same way you sent them, negatively. Now, you are most probably wondering something like, "How can I defend myself against the school bully if not by using negative magic?" Well you can, that is the beauty of magic—it's how you use it that counts.

To deal with the school bully, some may light a few black candles and wish that person harm. Now, that is negative magic. With positive magic, you can light a white candle, wish for the bully to leave you alone, and move on.

You do not need to practice negative magic when positive magic works even better, and the perk is that you will always stay in karma's good books, because those who are true practitioners believe and respect the oath:

> *Harm none for if you do, it will came*
> *back to you threefold.*

Magic in itself works in mysterious ways, and if a spell is performed in a negative manner, to cause harm, manipulate others, or change someone's destiny, you are asking for trouble and playing with the powerful forces of the universe.

Black and white, positive and negative, male and

female, you must be able to understand both, to be in tune with the forces of nature and the universe.

Search your heart, look deep into your soul, find your true self, and you will never disturb the balance between you and nature. Above all, never inflict your will on others, and if you still haven't figured it out, try following this principle:

> *If you don't like someone doing it to you, don't do it to others.*

chapter three

Witches

When I was growing up, I used to watch through peepholes as my father practiced his own craft, which always fascinated me. He worked with a lot of candles and herbs—always adding this or that to some spell or herbal medicine he was working on for someone. His practice always left me spellbound, and it still does to this day.

I remember clients constantly coming in and out of our house from the "spiritual room," as he called it. The spiritual room had a small table with three chairs. A sharp scent of cologne was always in the air. White candles would be lit, and dry herbs could always be found in dozens of shoeboxes, all labeled for easy access. In every house my parents lived in over the years, the spiritual room always smelled and looked the same way.

From a young age I was very attracted to what I used to call *brujeria*, which is Spanish for "witchcraft." I wanted to take my father's beliefs and combine them with my own eclectic beliefs about *brujeria* and witchcraft, discovering different things and mixing them all together to come out with good results. And that was what I did, thanks to his guidance and teachings.

I love being a witch, but I especially love being a solitary witch, rather than part of a coven, because it allows me to be flexible in the art of spellmaking and to do my own rituals without anyone else looking over my shoulder. This allows me to express my beliefs and feelings to the only ones who really matter—my God and Goddess. I've always loved to mix natural energies together to produce positive results for any given situation, and to help others with their dreams and goals.

People believe witches are the only ones who can do spells and tap into universal energies, but this is not true. Anyone can reach out to the universe to make their dreams a reality, just as a witch can—it is just a matter of having the right frame of mind. Never say, "It will not happen." Always stay positive, and never let a negative thought penetrate to your subconscious mind. Always say things in a positive way, such as: "It will happen." In the process, see it happening in your mind, and play it back over and over again, like a movie! This will strengthen your focus on a positive outcome.

The world has the wrong concept about witches, thanks to Hollywood, which has made us look ugly and evil in about 95 percent of its movies and cartoons. This is far from the truth. We witches are not ugly, evil, or weird. We witches are mysterious. Some of us are writers, while others are models, doctors, lawyers, and members of a variety of other professions. You may not know we are witches because it's not the way we dress that makes us witches, but the way we carry the craft in our hearts.

The true witch is a physician of the heart, a specialist in spirituality, meditation, and positive visualization. A little bit of this herb, or that oil, is the key to fulfillment of the witch's craft.

Witches are in tune with nature and those around them. The most gratifying aspect of being a witch is being able to aid others in their time of need. Many people call witches the best counselors around. Witches do not tell you to take an aspirin for your headache, but to light a blue candle, run a little bit of lemongrass oil around your temples, and search for the reason for the sudden intrusion of pain into your life.

Witches are able to manifest their dreams with natural energies. They can heal others and themselves, if it is meant to be. Witches understand and protect the innocent. They have the gift of divination to find the answers others need, and to advise in matters of the heart.

Do not be misled. Look around you: There are real-life witches out there, but there are also trendy witches. If you are serious, carry the craft in your heart and not in the way you dress or wear your hair.

☆ Witches ☆

The faith in our God and Goddess is pure and true. To love nature is our code. To be true to friends and loved ones is a ritual we practice on a daily basis. We protect and respect every single living thing. We cherish the beauty around us and give thanks to Mother Earth for letting us share it with her.

If you don't know it yet, witchcraft is a true religion, and like any other religion, it deserves your respect, just as you would expect someone else to respect your own beliefs and convictions. It is not a game; witchcraft is as real as it gets.

We witches work with nature's natural energies— we light candles, affirming our intentions, or burn incense, or carry little bags full of herbs or crystals with us. This does not make us evil, but *mystical*.

Witchcraft has never been and should never be associated with anything Satanic. We witches do not believe in Satan. Witchcraft existed long before Christianity was born, and Satan is a Christian belief. The key to knowledge is to have an open mind and if in doubt, make the library your best friend and find your answers in the written knowledge of those who actually practice witchcraft and not in hearsay or others' misconceptions.

Keep your faith and beliefs within you—don't tell

the world about them until you are ready. Sometimes when doing a spell, other people's negativity can get in the way, so you may find it best to work by yourself. Not everyone out there understands magic or witchcraft, and some people like to judge anything they don't understand.

chapter four
The God and the Goddess

ou must know a little about the God and the Goddess to understand the nature of their presence in the craft. These deities are of Pagan origin. You may have been confused in the past because of the numerous gods and goddesses out there, but I will make it easier for you to understand. There is only one God and only one Goddess, but different cultures call them by different names, according to their own traditions, which could be from Greek, Celtic, Roman, or even from Egyptian mythology.

Remember when we talked about a positive and a negative? There is also male and female energy, which is the base of our existence and the essence behind the God and Goddess. I don't wish to put a specific identity on these two very important deities. You may like to do that on your own if you already know what tradition you're most affiliated with. If you have difficulty trying to visualize these powerful deities, you may be able to relate to them as I do.

The Goddess is the bright star in the sky, the full moon, the plants, the flowers, and the blue waters of the sea. She is the healer, the one who sits by your side and listens to your sadness and cries with you, as she understands the pain you are going through. She holds the hands of sick children all over the universe and brings comfort to those burdened with unanswered questions. The beauty of our planet is the silken, silver veil she wraps around us to bring comfort and peace to our existence, and if it is carelessly torn, she will bring nothing but chaos to those who destroy the beauty of her garment, the Earth. The Goddess must be respected. She is the crone who watches over us, the mother who gives us life, and the young teen who grants wishes if you will only believe.

The God, on the other hand, is the male energy. He is the warrior, the hunter, and the protector; the sun and the desert are his hunting grounds. At times forgotten by all, but always there in the background with his free, untamed animals, he is seen as a mighty stag, roaming the forest as he seeks the death of winter and the birth of spring. The God can also be as generous as the Goddess, but you will need to find that out for yourself. You have heard of "getting in touch with your feminine side." Well, you will need to get in touch with your masculine side to understand the God.

If you would like something to represent the Goddess on your altar, you may use a seashell, and for the God an acorn or even pine cones. The Goddess will give you spells for love and compassion, while the God gives strength and protection to the spells when needed.

Respect both and you will be blessed with their kindness and strength, their love and understanding—but most of all, with the beauty of knowing that they are living energies and are all around us, in every corner of our world. It is just a matter of being in tune with nature and everything around us.

May the God and Goddess always guide you.

chapter five
Getting Started:
Spells, Tools, and Rituals

Each living thing possesses an energy field, within and around it, that is filled with earthbound vibrations. When you combine those natural energies with a positive thought, you generate a high frequency out into the universe. Your needs are then suspended in cosmic dust, and the energy returns to you, always with positive results. This process is what I call a spell.

Spells belong to the mystical science. In spells, objects with natural energies are used, such as herbs, crystals, or candles, and much more. Each one represents and reinforces the art of positive magic, and these are what I call the tools needed to conduct a spell. Without these natural energies, a positive thought sent out to the universe is just a wish.

The tools are there to keep your focus on the task at hand. For example, suppose one of your friends has been ill for a while, and you wish to send him or her some healing energies. As you start to gather the tools needed for the healing spell, such as candles, herbs, or crystals, your mind is already focused on one thing, your friend!

Then there is the ritual, which is the art of sending your needs to the universe with words, feelings, and actions, such as lighting the candles at a certain time and saying a small phrase for the final climactic closing of the spell. Speaking the words out loud transmits your needs verbally to the universe, with strength.

The important three—spells, tools, and rituals—are best explained as:

· Spell: The art of visualizing your needs to the universe

· Tools: The gathering and use of natural energies to keep focused on your needs and intended results

· Ritual: The final climactic step after the spell and tools are together, to send your message out to the universe with power, sometimes using words that rhyme

Altar

When doing magical workings, it's important to have a quiet place to work. Let's call this place your altar, a holy space where you make your offerings to the universe or earthly powers, to aid your ritual. Just by sitting or standing in front of it, you are able to tune your thoughts to the purpose at hand.

To set up an altar is as easy as ABC. There is no need to fuss or bother, just find a small table. You can have the table in your room or somewhere in the house where you will not be disturbed while conducting your magical workings. A card table is a good idea, as you can fold it up when not in use. Or you can always leave the table up for your daily positive visualization or meditations—it's up to you.

If you are going to leave your altar up at all times, you may consider covering it with a simple cotton cloth. Some people prefer purple, black, or red cloth for strength in rituals, but the color really does not matter, I will leave it up to you and your own taste.

Then decorate it, make this your own sacred space. Use your beliefs to enhance your reasons for having an altar. Flowers are always welcome and bring a fresh approach to your magical working. Flowers can provide a sense of refreshment and purity, a space where you can find peace and comfort at any time of the day.

The other essential thing is two candleholders for your altar. One candleholder is for the God, and this will be a gold candle. The other is for the Goddess, a silver one. You may wish to keep the candles on your altar at all times and light them when conducting a spell, or simply when you need some time out to think things over.

There is no right or wrong way to create your altar. Our entire existence consists of experimentation and learning, and if anyone tells you different, then you know that he or she still has a lot of learning to do. Try different ways by mixing and matching. See what works for you. The universe knows your intentions are pure, and next time around you will be guided accordingly.

To purify your altar for magical workings, mix together a teaspoon each of dried rosemary, lavender, and rose petals, then sprinkle all over your altar. Follow this by lighting a white and a blue candle, and let them burn down until they are consumed. Then, light a frankincense incense stick and fan your altar with it. After this, your altar is ready for your magical workings.

Censer and Charcoal Tablets

A censer is a bowl in which a charcoal tablet can be lit. Dried herbs are placed on top of the lit charcoal to create the energies needed for your spells, which makes the bowl a natural incense burner. You can use any bowl for this purpose, a plain glass or ceramic bowl or whatever you feel will blend in with your other altar tools.

Once you have made that decision, fill the bowl with rock salt, sand, or dirt. This must be done to protect the bowl from the charcoal tablet, as once lit it becomes a very high fire hazard. If you accidentally drop the charcoal, pick it up immediately with a pair of tongs—*do not attempt to pick it up with your fingers*, as it can cause major burning to the skin.

When you are ready to light the charcoal tablet, place it on top of the rock salt, then go outside and light it. At first you will see grey smoke. After the smoke disperses, you can take the bowl indoors and place your herbs gently on top of the tablet, to commence or continue your spell.

Essential Oils and an Oil Burner

Essential oils are made out of actual herbs or other plants. There are many different pure essential oils on the market, but try to find a reasonably priced brand so it won't break your budget.

An oil burner is used to burn the essential oils. You can find an oil burner just about anywhere, and prices range from inexpensive to ridiculous. Just be sensible, pick up something nice and cheap. It will work wonders.

Caution: Tea lights and any other candles used for your ritual are never to be left unattended while you do a spell. Be aware of fire hazards at all times!

Little Drawstring Bags

You will be required to use a little drawstring bag of a specific color in some of the spells. You may be able to purchase them, but if unable to find one, you can actually make your own. Try to find a piece of cotton material, of the color specified for the spell, and about the size of a lady's handkerchief. Then tie it together, using a cotton string, a piece of yarn, or a leather thong, to keep the contents from falling out.

Parchment Paper

Parchment paper will also be used in some spells and can be purchased from most stationery outlets and crafts supplies stores. If unable to find it, you can do the following: Get a plain piece of 8 ½ x 11 paper and scrunch it up with both hands, then open it, smooth it out, and presto—instant parchment paper!

Always have **pens** handy—red, blue, and black. You will be using pens to write passages, as part of your spells. At times you may also require a **feather**. There is no need to go to a great expense here, just any large feather will do—from a duck or rooster, for instance—but if you actually take the feather from the bird, ask permission to do so. How would you like it if someone took what is yours without asking? If you follow this rule, you will be following the laws of karma.

Mortar and Pestle

A mortar and pestle are needed to crush and mix herbs together. These can be found at any good kitchenware store, just ask for them by name. Wooden or marble ones can be used. Be practical—you may even find a set that your mother has tucked away somewhere in the kitchen cupboard.

Crystals

Crystals provide spiritual enlightenment in our rituals and spells. There are hundreds of crystals out there that are a great asset to any magical workings. You should use them whenever possible to make a connection with Mother Earth.

From time to time you will be asked to wear a particular crystal or carry it in a drawstring bag. You can purchase crystals from just about anywhere these days, but if you're unable to find them, consult your nearest lapidary club, and they will be more than happy to help you find the one you need.

Cleansing

Crystals not only give out good vibrations; they can also absorb bad ones. Cleansing them before your magical workings will rid them of any unwanted energies and ready them for programming your needs to the universe.

There are many ways to cleanse crystals, from water to salt to sunlight. I have included in each spell that calls for a crystal, the most effective way to cleanse it.

Herbs

An herb is anything that grows above ground or underground, from flowers to weeds to all the spices above the kitchen sink. Any plant when dried becomes an herb. Some herbs are steeped in hot water, like tea leaves, and made into infusions, which can be sipped slowly to settle the stomach or to help us fall asleep. When an herb is burned on top of charcoal in your censer, it becomes incense for your spell, to create a needed effect.

Most health food stores carry a wide selection of herbs. But if you are unable to find an herb, try the closest nursery, ask for the actual plant, and take it home with you. Before taking what you need from the plant, always ask permission, then focus, and you will feel the plant speak to you. If all is clear, take a few leaves or a bit of a branch. Follow this by leaving a token of appreciation, like another seedling or a small crystal.

An herb must be dried before you can use it on your censer, and the process can sometimes take a few days, so always plan ahead by making sure you have all the tools you need to conduct the spell.

To dry the herb, leave your clippings on top of some brown paper or even newspaper, and place them in a shaded area, out of the sun. If you have more than the desired amount, bottle the remainder in a glass or plastic container and label it. This way you can use it again when needed, and you can start building your own herbal collection for your magical workings.

Candles

Candles are used in about 95 percent of all spells to enhance the desire and strength of the spell. The colors of candles are very important in any type of magical workings. Each color in the spectrum has a magical meaning and is used to promote and enhance that particular desire to the universe.

When you purchase a candle, make sure that it is the same color all the way through. If you use a blue candle for a spell and discover, when you light it, that it is white in the middle, then it is not the right candle to use for your magical workings. The reason for this is that you need that specific color to be portrayed to the universe. If the color is mixed, the universe will get mixed signals, and the spell will not work to its fullest potential.

This may sound a bit weird, but a candle needs to be "dressed" if you are using it for any magical purpose. Don't worry, you are not going to dress it with a t-shirt and hat. A candle is divided into two parts. The part from the middle up towards the wick is called the north pole, and from the middle down to the bottom is called the south pole. When a spell calls for dressing a candle, you must rub it with the oil specified in the spell, then rub a bit of the oil in both of your hands. The right hand goes from the center of the candle up its north pole, while the left hand goes from the center of the candle down the south pole, but never both at once in an up-and-down manner.

There is always a need for **candleholders** on your altar, so find some that you like. There is no need to go to great expense here, be practical. From time to time, you are going to have to clean old wax from the candleholders, and the simplest way to do this is just to run them under hot water. When you do this, make sure you have the plug in the sink to collect the wax, or you will have major drainage problems and a possible altercation with a parental figure!

Always keep fire safety in mind while using candles. Never leave them burning all night unattended, and when extinguishing a candle after you have finished the spell, do not blow it out. If you do, all the energy the candle was sending out into the universe will blow away, as if the spell had never been conducted in the first place. For this purpose try to find a candlesnuffer. You can use your fingers, but when you have to put out four or five candles at one time, it can get a little bit painful, so a snuffer is always a good idea. Try to remember, **Never blow, always snuff.**

Astral Color Candles

"Astral color" is the name given to a candle that is used in a spell for a specific person, according to that person's star sign. If a spell instructs you to light an astral color for a friend in need, find out your friend's star sign and then match it to a color, using the chart below:

Astral Colors

Star Sign	Dates	Color
Aries	Mar 21-Apr 19	White
Taurus	Apr 20-May 20	Red
Gemini	May 21-Jun 21	Red
Cancer	Jun 22-Jul 21	Green
Leo	Jul 22-Aug 22	Red
Virgo	Aug 23-Sept 22	Black
Libra	Sept 23-Oct 22	Black
Scorpio	Oct 23-Nov 21	Brown
Sagittarius	Nov 22-Dec 21	Gold
Capricorn	Dec 22-Jan 19	Red
Aquarius	Jan 20-Feb 18	Blue
Pisces	Feb 19-Mar 20	White

The Moon

You will notice that some of the spells in *Charm Spells* are performed during certain phases of the moon. The moon is a very important part of your magical workings. By paying attention to its phases, you will be able to enhance your magical efforts.

When the moon is bright and round and you can see in the dark, the moon is *full*. At this time the moon is at its greatest potential, and you will be able to conduct any type of spell.

Between the full moon and the new moon, the moon is *waning*, which means that it starts to decrease. This is a good time to work against any type of negative forces within yourself or others.

Then there is the *new* moon, and this moon cannot be seen. It is hidden and ready to start its new cycle. Once again, this is a good time for any type of spell.

Between the new moon and the full moon, the moon starts *waxing*, which means "growing." This is a good time to work on fulfilling your needs and wants, like health, wealth, love, and relationships. As the moon grows to its full potential, so do the things you need and want.

The best way to get to know the moon phases is to look at a calendar. Many calendars show the moon phases, and you should always consult one before performing spells.

Protection Prayer

When you are working against negative forces, it's always good to say a protection prayer before you start any spell. This will protect you from those who wish you mental and physical harm as well. You can use any prayer you wish, but if you don't have one, you may use the one I have been using for years whenever I conduct magic.

Protection Prayer

Divine universal forces,
Keep me safe.
Keep me out of harm's way
And protect me always
When I do my magical workings.

chapter Six
Mini Color Spells

Each individual color in the spectrum gives out a different frequency to our body and our everyday surroundings. Strong color vibrations are given out by the warm colors such as red and orange, while passive vibrations come from cool colors, like blues and pinks.

Color in magic has its advantages and should be used to convey your needs and wants to the universe when conducting a spell. So using color, whether it's in candles, the clothes you wear, or the little drawstring bag you keep your bits and pieces in, makes a stronger connection to the universe by enhancing your aura and making your needs clearer.

Below is a list of colors and their meanings, which you can use to help fulfill your needs, or to make your own spells. You can add color to your wardrobe or carry a colored cotton cloth with you at all times, for example. When you use color in this way, you are performing a mini spell. Use your imagination. As long as you know the meanings of the colors, anything is possible, and you can turn your dreams into reality.

Amber

You can use an amber crystal that has been cleansed

with frankincense essential oil for any type of psychic workings, such as learning to read the tarot or communicating with spirits, or you can hold the amber crystal while meditating, for deeper understanding.

Black

Black wards off negativity and can be used to remove hexes. It can be worn for protection and used to banish unwanted influences. You can even light a black and a white candle together to get rid of your own negativity.

Blue

Blue is the color of peace and protection. It calms emotions and protects you against negative forces. Blue is great to wear after illnesses to stabilize the physical body. People who have anger problems can wear blue, or you can light a blue candle to get rid of hidden anger and bring peace to the soul.

Gold

Gold strengthens the mind. It is the color that represents the God. Light a gold candle to communicate with your angels and to work on your money needs. Try to find some fake gold dust and frequently sprinkle it in the front yard to attract richness.

Green

Green is the color of growth, and also the color associated with money. It is the color of our planet, as it is forever growing. Green brings luck and aids the emotions. Light a green candle to acquire money or to heal emotional pain. Teens should wear green to stimulate their minds to learn and grow academically.

Indigo

Indigo is useful when working with the laws of karma. You can hold a lapis lazuli crystal while you meditate, to send your needs out to the universe, and also while performing psychic work.

Purple

Purple is used for spiritual development. In times of stress, light a lavender candle and place some lavender essential oil in your bath or under your pillow, to help when you're in need of sleep. Carry an amethyst crystal to aid an ongoing chronic physical condition or addiction.

Orange

Orange promotes encouragement. You can light an orange candle to meet new friends and communicate well with others. Orange is the color that honors words. Take an orange hankie to the library when you study, and you will remember the facts you always tend to forget.

Pink

As money is associated with green, love is with pink. Pink helps you make friends and keep your friends. It helps you love yourself so you can love others, and they are able to love you. Light a pink candle for a friend who is down in the dumps because of low self-esteem. You can even wear pink in your hair to attract a new love interest.

Red

Red enhances power and gives strength to your magical workings. Light a red candle when you feel you need answers from others or strength to face difficult situations. Wear red when you need energy to finish the day and feel whole again.

White

White is the color of the universe, purity, love, and understanding. If you seek answers, white will provide them. Light a white candle and ask your guardian angels for help. If you find yourself wronged by the universe, get a bunch of white flowers as an offering and ask karma the reason for the lessons you are learning. White is excellent for the sick and newborn babies because of its purity and tranquillity.

Yellow

Use yellow to cheer the soul and others around you. Yellow is for the solar plexus, the center of the gut feeling. If you are not listening to your gut instincts, wear yellow to help yourself hear them. Next time you buy a piece of clothing for your younger brother or sister, choose yellow to help them learn and grasp as much as they can in their early learning years.

chapter Seven
A Spell to Go, Please!

Spells to go" are a simple way to make your needs known to the universe. There are no rituals, just positive visualization and a few natural energies added to enhance your positive thoughts to the universe. I call them "spells to go" because that is what they really are—simple, straight to the point, with no extra fuss or bother. The only thing to remember is to use your positive visualization, which is the key to this simple way of conveying your needs to the universe. So play with spells to go as many times as you want, to bring about a needed change, to fulfill a desire, and even to help others in their time of need.

You can do the visualization at any time—before going to school in the morning, for instance, or after school. There is no time when you cannot do them.

Try to stay focused whenever you attempt them, and remember you must be willing and believing. This is the key to manifestation through positive visualization, for getting what your heart desires.

Spells to Go

Matchmaker

Tell your friends to get a teaspoon of dry basil leaves and a rose quartz crystal and keep them in a little pink drawstring bag, to make their dream guy or girl come around.

Money for a Date

Go to the supermarket (or a health food store, if necessary) and buy some chamomile tea. If you want to de-stress before the date, make yourself a cup. If you want $$$$ to treat your date, put some of the tea leaves inside your wallet.

Friends 4 Ever

Keep a bloodstone in your locker or backpack to find and make new friends who will last a lifetime.

Love Me Forevermore

Get two tiger's-eye crystals and leave them on the grass under a full moon for one night. Give one to the one you love and leave the other under your pillow, and forevermore there will be love.

I Am Who I Am

Burn a pink and a blue candle on a Monday night for the real you to be revealed, and for others to accept you as you are.

Heart Be True and Tell My Love

Dip your index finger into honey and draw an imaginary heart around your heart. This will send the message to the one you love.

Exam Jitters

A blue hankie will keep the jitters away so you can relax and do your best on the exam.

Just Enough

Always keep a bowl of rice with a citrine crystal in your kitchen for the simple everyday material needs.

Does Someone Have a Crush on You?

Carry seven balm-of-Gilead buds in a little red drawstring bag to attract the one you want to have around.

Dream Love

Just one drop of jasmine essential oil on top of your pillow will help you dream about and manifest the love you are seeking.

Cream and Sugar

"Mom and Dad, I'm so sorry!" Bring a bunch of white and yellow flowers to the house, and the apology you are offering will be accepted.

Two Hearts That Beat as One

From a fresh bunch of basil, crush a few leaves in your hands and use the oily substance to anoint the pulse points on your body. When your heart beats, it will send signals to the one you are in love with.

Lucky You

Feed the birds, and you will have the most amazing luck. You just have to ask, and you will receive.

Money Does Grow on Trees

Keep and eat cashews when money is needed—or for any other financial assistance.

Guys in Love

This may hurt, but if you want love you will do it, no matter what. Inside your shoes keep apple and pear seeds, and you shall see. . . .

Girls in Love

Sprinkle rose petals and a few fresh rosemary leaves in your shoes, and you will be loved more deeply than ever before, by a guy who's true to you.

Girlfriend, You Need Money?

Place a few copper coins (pennies will do) in a little clear bowl, then cover them with honey and sesame seeds to bring the money in. Your girlfriend will be pleased!

Should I or Shouldn't I?

Having problems making decisions? Then light an orange candle and meditate to find the right choice, then act upon it before midnight.

Be a Trendsetter

Mix dried violet leaves and white rose petals together and carry them in a pink drawstring bag, to get others to like your unique style.

Do Your Parents Need Money?

Fill two little brown drawstring bags with unsalted peanuts and corn. Your mother needs to carry one in her handbag, and your father should leave one in the glove compartment of the family car.

Love Note

After you finish writing your love note, sprinkle about half a teaspoon of crushed cardamom seeds on top, let it sit for a few minutes, then blow them to the wind in the direction of your love. You will receive a reply that's ever so sweet.

Superstar

To be popular is easy, but to be kind at the same time takes a person who's good at heart. Carry a bloodstone crystal with you, and you will always be a legend in their eyes.

☆ A Spell to Go, Please! ☆

A Wish in the Clouds

Blow a small handful of sage toward a large cloud and make a wish for the desires you carry in your heart.

Job Catcher

Need a part-time job? Chop a bunch of parsley and add it to your bath, and you will never look back.

Home Sweet Home

To keep your home always filled with love, mix lavender with your carpet deodorizer and sprinkle away any time your home needs some Tender Loving Care.

Money to Burn

Go to four banks and get a withdrawal slip from each one. Take them home and do an imaginary withdrawal with each one, as if you had bank accounts at all four banks. Take fifty dollars out of each bank, then burn all the slips at the same time and make a money wish to last a lifetime.

Sweetness Forever

Always wash your hair with shampoos that are made from flower essences. This will make sure love flows through you—even through your hair!

Shell It Out

Keep a pecan nut with you for your money needs—but don't eat it, please!

Diary Be True

Keep red rose petals in your diary or journal, and the words of love you write will come true.

Terminator or If I Only Had the Nerve

For the courage and strength to face the challenges you wish would just go away, get an orange and insert an aquamarine crystal deep within it. Keep it in your room, and before you leave the house, hold it and wish for the courage you need, and you shall find it.

Invitation to Cupid

Tie a knot in a yard of pink silk ribbon and leave it hanging by the end of your bed. When Cupid comes around, he takes the ribbon and wraps it around the one he knows will love you very much.

Feel Better, Mom

Bring your mother a fresh bunch of white carnations to help her through the flu or any other illness that is making her feel blue.

☆ A Spell to Go, Please! ☆

Say Every Night to Find True Love

I'm dreaming away for the guy
*   I praise and on the way I awake,*
Love hearts are in the air, and my guy is there.
Romantic dinners and beach walks at sunrise,
*   hot summers are on the way,*
Here we go again, love is on the way
So don't despair.

(By Beverly)

The Sooner the Better

Don't say, "I'm going to have money someday." Instead
say, "I will be rich when I'm twenty-three," and you will
be, if you believe.

Watch Your Words

Never say, "I'm broke!" For if you do, you will be so forever.

Chick Magnet

Keep a girl's hair clip in your bookbag or backpack, and
this will attract the girl you always wanted and never
could have.

Sweet Harmony

To stop friends from disagreeing, keep apple blossoms
around when friends get together.

Parties "R" Us

To have a fun party, burn two drops of lime and three drops of sweet orange essential oils together in your oil burner for scent, and make a citrus punch to serve your guests. At the end of the night, people will be asking when you are going to have another party.

Just Say, "No Way!"

This is a spell to keep the drug pusher away from you or your friends. With a pin, engrave the name of the drug pusher on a blue candle and stick it in the freezer. But remember, you can always simply say, "No."

Pretty Am I

Wrap pink and red ribbon around a few pieces of straw. They must be small so you can have them with you to feel beauty within, and much more.

Crystal Therapy

To help a friend suffering from cancer, give him or her an amethyst crystal and a warm, heartfelt hug.

Home Is Where the Heart Is

To stop your parents from fighting with each other, keep a rose quartz crystal in their bedroom. Or to stop them from fighting with you, keep a rose quartz crystal in your room!

☆ A Spell to Go, Please! ☆

The Veil of Beauty

To make your friend like herself, get a picture of her and cover it with a pink silk cloth. This will make her feel the love that only comes from deep within one's own soul.

New School

The night before you start at your new school, take a bath and add a cup of pineapple juice to the bathwater. Stay in the bath for about ten minutes. Then in the morning, as you walk into the school, chew on a piece of cinnamon stick. This will help you to be well liked, and kids will be asking you to hang around with them.

My Strength Is Your Strength

Hold the hand of the friend who needs your strength, then, with eyes closed, visualize a red flash of light penetrating your friend's heart. This will give your friend the strength he or she needs to fight.

Driver's Ed

When you are ready to take the driving test, take an aquamarine crystal with you, and you will soon be driving your friends around with you. Please, don't drink and drive—but if you do drink, just stay overnight, or call Mom and Dad to pick you up with no questions asked.

A Spark of Love

To spark the interest of someone in your school, carry the leaves of a willow tree in a little yellow drawstring bag, and you will see. . . .

Life Can Be Sweet

Get a glass bowl and fill it with candy sprinkles. Inside, place the name of the person who needs a bit of happiness in his or her life.

Fairy Talk

If you wish to talk to fairies, go out into the night with a bowl of milk, sit on the grass, and close your eyes—you will hear them walking and whirring around.

Self-Defense

Carry half a teaspoon of mugwort in a little blue drawstring bag, to feel protected from the ones who wish you physical harm after school.

Security System

Hang a head of garlic from a red ribbon behind the front door of your home.

☆ A Spell to Go, Please! ☆

Fresh Start

Write the fresh start you are wishing for on a piece of paper, then burn it and blow the ashes to the sea. If not the sea, a river will do nicely. Make sure it is windy so your wish can reach the forces where fresh starts are found.

A Is for Apple

Bring a nice bowl of apples for the teacher who gives you things to think about, and he/she will help you understand the subjects you need to learn at school.

Blast from the Past

At night, burn a frankincense incense stick, then close your eyes and try to remember your whole day backwards. This will strengthen the mind. It's not easy, so just take your time and do it as many times as you need to get it right.

chapter Eight
Spells and Rituals:
The Adventure Begins

Snagging That Hot Babe

Hot like chili peppers this person is,
and to catch him/her do this!

You will need:

1 white bowl	1 lemon
1 regular tea bag	3 cinnamon sticks
7 cooking cloves	1 teaspoon of sugar

Sprinkle the sugar in the white bowl, open the tea bag, and then sprinkle the tea leaves on top of the sugar. As you do this, think only of the babe you wish to reel in.

On the actual lemon write the name of his/her star sign, with only thoughts of this person in mind. Do not use personal names, just in case the universe has a different name in mind.

Insert the seven cooking cloves into the lemon, making a circle of them around the star sign. Follow this by placing the lemon in the middle of the bowl.

Make a triangle around the lemon with the cinnamon sticks, and say:

> Like a fish in the ocean,
> I'm going to reel you in,
> It's going to be the biggest
> and hottest catch,
> This town has ever seen.

Leave the bowl out on a full-moon night for one night.
Then place it under your bed without touching it for
seven nights. After the seventh night, on a Friday
night, bury it outside the hot babe's house.

≋

Wish Away

A wish does come true—if you believe in fairies, that is!
You will need:

- 10 walnuts (small)
- 10 bamboo shoots (small)
- 1 small rose quartz crystal
- 1 sage incense stick
- 1 orange candle (dress it with olive
  or lavender oil)

Light the orange candle, at any time of the day, and
make a wish without any personal gain for you or
anyone else, then say:

> Wishes do come true,
> if from the heart they are felt.

Follow this by making a circle around the candle with
the walnuts, then the bamboo shoots. In the middle,
next to the candle, place the rose quartz crystal. Light
and burn the sage incense stick while visualizing your
wish as real as it can possibly be.

Snuff the candle after ten minutes, and repeat this part of the ritual every day for seven days. Light the same candle and once again burn a sage incense stick, while visualizing your wish for ten minutes.

After the seventh day, take the walnuts, bamboo shoots, and rose quartz crystal out into your front yard and, as you lay them on the lawn, say:

> Fairy realm, here I leave a token
> for the wish made in secrecy,
> Eat the walnuts and feast upon them,
> Build new homes from the shoots
> as tall as you possibly can make them,
> May the rose quartz bring
> love and peace upon you all,
> This I give to you
> for the wish you now hold.

Under no circumstances are you to tell anyone the wish, and do not promise the fairies anything for the wish—they are mischievous at times, so take care and do this spell exactly as it is written.

≋

Attention Seeker

Unnoticed I have been, no longer will I be.

You will need:

    1 handful of thyme

    7 cherry pits

    1 jasmine incense stick

    1 small handful of coriander

    1 red candle (dress with lavender oil)

    The petals of 1 red rose

Draw a warm bath, light the red candle, and burn the jasmine incense inside your bathroom, while thinking about being noticed by all who are around.

Follow this by sprinkling the barley sugar, the coriander, the seven cherry pits, and lastly the petals of the red rose into the bathwater.

Submerge yourself in the bath, visualizing yourself as a cheerful, caring person, listening to and understanding friends who come to you for good advice. The key to being noticed is to feel good about who you really are. Exhibit this, and you should be noticed for the rest of your life, whenever the sun or moon is out.

Stay in the bath for about twenty minutes. Your hair must also get wet, and you must not rinse off after the spell for a whole day. Pat yourself dry—this way you are sealing the energy within you.

Do this on a Wednesday at any time you like, as frequently as you like.

≋

Needle and Thread

When a heart is broken, mending must be done.

You will need:

    1 rose quartz crystal necklace

    7 white flowers (of any kind)

    1 blue candle (dress with baby oil)

    1 pink candle (dress with baby oil)

    The petals of 2 red roses

    A piece of parchment paper

    A needle and pink thread

Draw a heart on the parchment paper, then tear the heart in half while visualizing the pain you carry inside.

Light the pink candle to bring peace of mind, then the blue candle to heal the pain in your heart.

Sprinkle the rose petals around the candles, and place the necklace in the middle. Thread your needle and sew the heart together. With each stitch, you are mending yourself within, so say:

> I am mending my broken heart
> and I will be fine,
> Matters of the heart are hard to face,
> But face this pain I must
> so I can heal the hurt inside.

Draw a happy face and some sunshine rays on your now mended heart, and then write this out:

I am OK

Leave the heart in the middle of the candles, and do not remove it until both candles are consumed right to the very end. Follow this by putting on the rose quartz necklace, then go outside and burn your now mended heart. Blow the ashes away into the night, and no longer will you hurt inside.

Sweet Sugar Pie

I will seek high and low for a sweetheart to love.
You will need:

1 teaspoon of cinnamon powder
1 pink candle, with a holder (dress the
    candle with lemongrass essential oil)
12 little pebbles
1 cup of water in a small bowl
1 cup of rock salt in a small bowl
1 pink drawstring bag
1 rose incense stick, with a holder

On a full-moon night when the stars are out, go outside barefoot and follow these directions properly.

Visualize a circle and walk into the middle of this

imaginary circle. Place the bowl of water in front of you. On your right, light and stand the pink candle. Then on your left, light and stand the rose incense stick. Finally, place the bowl of rock salt behind you. You have just placed the four elements around you, and they are ready to find the sweetie pie you wish for.

Next, make a circle around you with the twelve little pebbles, each one representing one of the twelve star signs of the zodiac. Hold your hands out to the Goddess and say out loud:

> I seek a love in my life,
> one who is true and will love me true,
> Pebbles, no matter the star sign,
> start searching for my
> sweetheart tonight.

Sit inside your imaginary circle visualizing the guy/girl you wish to attract. Do not use names—the universe knows better than you, who will love you true.

Gather each pebble and place them all in the little pink drawstring bag. Keep the bag under your pillow until your sweetheart enters your life.

≋

Revenge Is Sweet...Not!!!

Positive magic is the only way.

You will need:

> 1 piece of parchment paper
> 1 black candle (dress with olive oil)
> 1 pink candle (dress with olive oil)
> 1/2 yard of blue ribbon
> 1 teaspoon of salt
> 1 red-ink pen

On the piece of parchment paper, write the name of the person who has done you harm, using the red-ink pen. Also write down the things that the person has done to disturb you or your friends so much.

Fold the paper four times and light the black candle as you say:

> You hurt me, but I wish you no harm,
> I just wish your negative energy
> to be gone from my sight.
> The universe knows of your injustice
> and the day will come,
> When you will have to stand trial,
> For the wrongs you have done.

Light the pink candle and say:

> Love I send you, go in peace,
> I will always be a better person

> than you could ever possibly be,
> For the good of all if it's to be,
> You will never bother my friends or me.

Sprinkle the salt on the paper and then tie three knots in the blue ribbon. As you do this, say:

> You will never harm anyone again,
> Not even yourself, and you will see
> the wrongs and the pain you inflict.

Bury this bundle on the right side of your house, and only dig it up after you see proof right in front of your eyes that this person is now nice as pie.

Enemy Be Gone

Don't you wish they'd leave you alone?

You will need:

1 pair of scissors	1 frankincense incense
1 tiger's-eye crystal	stick
1 cup of rice	1 bowl
1 blue candle (dress	Basil
with coconut oil)	

Some paper with your enemy's handwriting on it

Burn the frankincense incense stick and light the blue candle, while thinking of the one who does you harm, someone you want out of your life.

Empty the cup of rice into the bowl, and say:

> Each grain represents a day in my life,
> You will not harm me for a very long time.

Place the paper on top of the rice, then say:

> Here is the imprint of your hand,
> Which will never stand against me again.

Sprinkle basil on top of the paper, then say:

> Protected I feel and I shall be.

Place the tiger's-eye crystal on top, then open the scissors and place them on top of the bowl, and say:

> Be gone enemy of mine forever more,
> You will finally leave me alone.

Place this bowl in your room and keep it for as long as this person stays in your way.

Babe Magnet

*All it takes is a magnet to attract
the one you would like to date.*

You will need:

    1 pink cotton cloth for your altar table
    1 small magnet
    1 pin

2 pink candles (dress with olive oil)
7 small bay leaves
Seeds from a pear you have eaten
1 handful of rose petals
1 yellow drawstring bag
A few drops of pure essential lavender oil
Censer with a charcoal block

Light both of the candles, while thinking only of the one you wish to have and to hold. Light your censer and sprinkle the dry rose petals over it, while thinking about capturing this new love.

Hold the magnet in your right hand and the pin in your left, and say:

> I am the magnet, he/she is the pin.

Bring the magnet and the pin closer together until connection is made and felt. Hold the magnet and pin over one of the candle flames and say:

> Connection is made.

Bring the magnet and pin over the censer and let the smoke carry your thoughts to the universe, while saying three times:

> Smoke of love
> bind us together forevermore.

Place the magnet and pin, the pear seeds, the essential lavender oil, and the bay leaves inside the yellow drawstring bag. Hold the bag over the smoke and say:

> Captivated you will be,
> metal to magnet shall we be.
> Never to be apart,
> I will captivate your heart.

Let the candles burn out, and leave your now captivating little pouch under your pillow for seven nights, and then carry it with you at all times.

Hook, Line, and Sinker
We all want to love, be loved, and keep love.
You will need:

- 2 tiger's-eye crystals
- 1 clear glass
- 2 pink candles (dress the candles with lavender oil)
- 1 pink drawstring bag
- 1 blue drawstring bag
- 1 handful of dill seeds
- 1 yard of pink ribbon
- 2 pieces of parchment paper
- 1 teaspoon of salt

To cleanse the two tiger's-eye crystals, place them in

the clear glass, fill it with water, and add the salt. Leave it outside for three days and three nights. Then, when you are ready to conduct the spell, light the two pink candles while visualizing the love you wish to hold.

Put one of the tiger's eye crystals and half of the dill seeds in the blue drawstring bag, then write down your name on a piece of parchment paper and place it inside the blue bag, too. On the other piece of parchment paper, write a description of the personality and physical appearance of the one you like, but do not use that person's name. Insert the paper in the pink bag with the other tiger's-eye and the rest of the dill seeds.

Bind the two bags together with the pink ribbon and tie seven knots. As you tie each one of the knots, say:

> Be it you the one I like,
> Or the new love the universe
> has around the corner,
> Together we are to stay, our love will last,
> Until the universe has its day.

Bury both of the bags under a rosebush or buy a rose and bury it somewhere with the bags, and then dig up the bags in seven days and put them away in a happy place.

Pressure Cooker

Be yourself, and if others don't like you,
then who needs them anyway?

You will need:

    1 aquamarine crystal
    1 seed of a peach you have eaten
      (let it dry for three days out in the sun)
    10 sunflower seeds
    1 red drawstring bag
    3 pieces of frankincense tear incense
    Charcoal on your censer

Light the charcoal on your censer, then add the three pieces of frankincense tear incense. Hold the aquamarine crystal over the smoke in order to seek the strength to drive peer pressure away.

Place the peach seed, the sunflower seeds, and the crystal in the drawstring bag. Hold the bag over the smoke and say:

> Hold fast, let this day be the day I will
> not allow peer pressure to govern me.
> I like who I am, I am me, like me or not,
> I know what's best for me.

Wear the drawstring bag at all times, and peer pressure will be a thing of the past.

☰

Zip It

Don't you just hate gossip?

You will need:

    1 piece of parchment paper

    7 cooking cloves

    Sandalwood powder

    1 large safety pin

    Small square black cloth

On the parchment paper, write the name of the person spreading nasty gossip around.

Open the black cloth and place the name on top, sprinkle sandalwood powder over the person's name, and put the seven cooking cloves on top. As you close the bundle with the safety pin, say:

> Your tongue is darkened
> by your spiteful nature,
> Find something better to do,
> you will not spread
> malicious rumors ever again.

Keep this little black cloth in a special place, where no one can touch or hold it for at least seven days. Then let the water of a stream carry it away, and zipped forever that person will be.

The Truth Must Be Known
Speak the truth forevermore.

You will need:

    1 red candle (dress with olive oil)
    1 pinch of black pepper
    1 pinch of cumin powder
    1 piece of red paper

Light the red candle on a Wednesday night, with thoughts of the truth that needs to be told. Sprinkle black pepper around the candle and say:

> Your mouth will tingle
> until the truth unfolds.

Then sprinkle cumin powder on top of the black pepper and say:

> The taste will last
> until the truth comes out.

Let the candle burn down all the way. Blow the powders into the wind, and you should hear the truth you seek.

Protected I Will Be
Protection is needed, and I will seek it!

You will need:

    1 myrrh incense stick
    1 black drawstring bag

1 Apache tear crystal

1 teaspoon of mint leaves

1 garlic clove

1 blue candle (dress with almond oil)

Light the blue candle, while thinking about the protection you seek. Then light the myrrh incense stick and hold the Apache tear crystal over the smoke while you say:

> Behold, protection I seek and need,
> Oh, our divine Goddess, help me and
> protect me please from things I have
> no control over in the
> next few weeks.

Insert the mint leaves, the garlic clove, and the Apache tear crystal into your little bag, and keep it with you at all times.

Dreams

Let us keep the good ones and get rid of the bad ones.

You will need:

1 white cottonball

1 teaspoon of mouthwash

Splash cold water on your face first thing when you awake and recall your dream. If it was a good dream, one you wish to keep, trace the sleep lines on your face with the cottonball, and forever the dream will stay.

If you had a nightmare and you do not want it to come true, fill the sink with warm water and add the mouthwash. Rinse your face with the warm water, and the dream will be washed away from the sleep lines on your face and will not return to haunt you ever again.

Something to remember about dreams: If you describe your good dreams to a friend you trust after midday and describe your bad ones before midday, the good dreams you will keep, and the bad ones will go straight back to the bottom of the sea, and no longer will they be real.

Aphrodite's Glow

A loving change I need,
and I will make my aura the loving pink of silk.

You will need:

    1 glass bottle with a top

    1 pink silk cloth

    3 rosebuds

    1 yard of pink silk ribbon

    1 rose quartz crystal

    1/4 teaspoon of pink food coloring

    1 cup of distilled water

This is best done on a full-moon night. Cleanse the

rose quartz crystal under cool running water, then place it inside the glass bottle with the distilled water and the pink food coloring, and close the bottle with the lid.

Follow this by laying the bottle down on top of the pink cloth, and then sprinkle the petals of the three rosebuds around it. As you do this, visualize the love and energy you wish to have at all times, and the loving energies you have been missing every day.

Wrap the bottle and the rose petals with the pink cloth. Once this is done, tie the pink ribbon around the cloth to keep it in place.

Take this outside and lay it down gently in the moonlight. Then say:

> Lady of the night,
> shine on my bottle tonight,
> Fill it with love so I may attract
> those who care for me
> and are true to my soul.

First thing in the morning, bring the bottle in, unwrap it, and drink the water (but be careful not to swallow the rose quartz crystal). As you drink this loving pink potion, which is now a gift from the lady of the night, know that you will always project Aphrodite's Glow and be loved by everyone.

≋

Act Your Age
Grow up and shut up!

You will need:

  1 piece of parchment paper

  1 amethyst crystal

  1 blue candle (dress it with almond oil)

  1 pencil

  1 eraser

  1 sandalwood incense stick

On the parchment paper, write the name of the person you wish would grow up. Then write down what kind of growing up that person needs to be doing, and the things that are stopping his/her personal growth. Then light the blue candle and say:

> Find your own personal growth.

Using the eraser, rub out the things that are stopping this person's personal growth, and say:

> No longer will you do childish things,
> and a responsible teen you will be.

Light the incense and hold the piece of parchment paper in the smoke, then run the paper over the crystal. Wrap the parchment paper around the crystal, and then leave it out under the waxing moon for one night.

  Throw away the paper and give the crystal to the

person you are helping to grow, and the changes will begin to show.

≋

Trust in Me

Trust is earned.

You will need:

> 3 sunflower seeds
>
> 1 blue candle (dress with lemongrass essential oil)
>
> 1 white candle (dress with lemongrass essential oil)
>
> 5 large marshmallows
>
> 1 teaspoon of superfine sugar (available in the baking aisle of supermarkets)
>
> 1 plate
>
> Mortar and pestle

Light the blue and white candles together, then gently place the five marshmallows on the plate and put them in front of the candles. Crush the sunflower seeds with your mortar and pestle, while you say:

> Trust me, I wish you no harm,
> Hurt you were and trust must be earned.
> I will hold you in my arms,
> Wish you sweet dreams, and
> Be there anytime you need someone
> To listen and to trust your dreams with.

Then, sprinkle the crushed sunflower seeds around the outside of the marshmallow plate, and sprinkle the sugar on top.

Leave the candles lit for about half an hour, then take the marshmallows to the person who is in need of your trust, and have him/her eat one. You can also eat one if you wish. You will see the trust develop.

(This spell could be very manipulative, so please use the right words. This person needs to be able to trust you, so don't betray that trust—he/she has already been hurt before.)

Second Chance
Grounded I was, and the lesson was learned.
You will need:

    1 teaspoon of ground ginger

    1 regular tea bag

    1 teaspoon of dried rosemary

    4 bay leaves

    1 teaspoon of raw brown sugar

    Mortar and pestle

Go into the family kitchen and see if you can find all of the above. Mix the ground ginger with the contents of the tea bag. While you do this, with your mortar and pestle, visualize your grounding as over and done with. Add the bay leaves, crush them as small as you can, and last of all, add the raw brown sugar and the dried rosemary leaves.

Mix well and, when ready, pour the mixture into your bathtub and take a bath. You must bathe in this mixture from head to toe and let its scent soothe you. As you do, sit and think. Visualize the wrong you have done to get yourself grounded.

A lesson you have learned, and another chance from the universe is all you want, with a promise not to commit the wrong a second time. If you do, there will not be another chance the next time around.

Best Friends' Oath

Best friends are forever—male, female, or both together—as long as you are true to each other, and always love one another.

You will need:

> White silk ribbon, about a yard long
> White candle (dress in lavender oil),
>   with candleholder
> A little box filled with dried flowers
> A small personal item from each person
>   (this could be jewelry, a toy, anything
>   that means a lot to the person)

　　　1 large red apple
　　　1 red-ink pen

Make sure you are able to do this on a full-moon night with no rain in sight. Get your friends together, and ask each of them to wear a white outfit and bring a white ribbon, a white candle dressed in lavender with a holder, and a personal item.

　　　Go into the night, you and your friends all dressed in white, and make a circle. You should all hold the candle in your right hand and the ribbon in your left. Each of you should place the personal item by your feet.

　　　The small box filled with dried flowers, the apple, and the pen must be placed in the center of the circle. Once everything is in place, you are ready to begin.

　　　Light one of the candles and pass it around to light each and every one of the others. Try not to let the wind blow it out, as you must use the same flame to light all the rest. After all the candles are lit, everyone is to say:

> Light of darkness, darkness of light,
> friends we are, and
> friends we will forever remain.

Each candle is then placed about a foot in front of each person.

　　　Then pick up the pen and get each person to write his/her full name on the white ribbon he/she brought.

As each one writes, that person is to say:

> My name is who I am,
> our friendship is sacred,
> Sacred as the name I was given
> on the date of my birth,
> I will treasure our friendship,
> A bond made this night
> will endure within me for
> the rest of time.

As each of you finishes, place the ribbon by your feet.

The apple is then passed around, and each person must take a bite. The last bite must leave only the actual core, which will be the center of eternal friendship. Braid all the ribbons together to make one. Place the apple core in the box, together with the ribbons and the personal item each brought along.

Close the box. Each of you must hold your candle up high with both hands, while you say together:

> Friends for life and the hereafter
> we shall forever remain.

The box then is passed around and kept for a month at each one of the friends' houses. If by chance one wishes not to remain faithful to the rest, the ribbon and the personal item are given back with no hard feelings.

If by chance that person wishes to come back, all the others must agree, and the group must initiate that person once again—but this can only be done after six months and one day from the day he or she departed from the group.

Easy Cash

Need money? Let's go get some.

You will need:

- 1 piece of green paper
- 1 pen with green ink
- 1 scissors
- 1 green candle (dress with virgin olive oil)
- 1 celery stick, and a knife to cut it with
- 1 bunch of fresh basil

Cut the piece of green paper into the size of a fifty-dollar bill. In the top-right and bottom-left corners, write $50, in numerals. Light the green candle while visualizing your purse or wallet never being empty. No mothballs here!

Cut the celery stick in small pieces and place them on top of your new fifty-dollar bill. Pick a few of the leaves out of the bunch of basil and squeeze the natural oil out of the leaves with your hands, then smear it on the bill.

As you do this, say:

> My purse/wallet will always have money,
> Never going out, but always coming in.

Take this new green fifty-dollar bill and keep it in
your purse or wallet at all times, and you will see....

Pass with Flying Colors

*Exams are hard, so let's do a spell to help
you absorb all the info you've learned!*

You will need:

    1 citrine crystal

    Dried rosemary

    1 yellow candle (dress with rosemary essential oil)

    1 orange candle (dress with rosemary essential oil)

    1 yellow drawstring bag

Light the yellow and orange candles—this will help
you concentrate and make your brain assimilate and
retain all the words that you have read. You can light
yellow and orange candles any time you need help
with your everyday homework or study program.

Place the dried rosemary and the citrine crystal in
the little yellow drawstring bag, and take it with you
on the exam day. It will help activate the learning you
have done—and it wouldn't hurt to tell your mother,

father, or whoever is home to light orange and yellow candles for you on the day of the exam, just to keep things on that level for you.

≋

I Wish You Could Be in My Shoes
Help your parents understand that you are a teen.
You will need:

    1 lavender incense stick

    2 white candles (dress with coconut oil)

    A handful of rose petals

    A picture of you and your parents alone
       together (do not cut anyone out of the
       picture)

On a Wednesday, at a time when there is peace and quiet in the house, light the lavender incense stick, and then light both white candles. Place the picture between the white candles and, as you sprinkle the rose petals around the picture, say:

> Understand my teen years,
> as you once wished your parents did.
> Love me for who I am and not
> for who you want me to be,
> I am myself, and that is who I wish to be.

Let the candles burn down right to the very end, and

you will see a change within days. But remember, your parents do want what is best, so listen to them and never forget their advice, which in years to come you will "download."

Show Me the Money

Money means numbers, and numbers need adding.
You will need:

A five-dollar bill

2 blue candles

2 green candles

1 teaspoon of dried mint leaves

1 tablespoon of olive oil

On a Thursday morning go to your bank and withdraw only a five-dollar bill. When you get home, place the bill on top of your altar, and mix the mint leaves and the olive oil together on a small plate. Then dress your candles with this money mixture, and light them.

Follow this by visualizing the note multiplying in front of your eyes, and say:

$$5 + 5 + 5 + 5 = 20$$
$$20 + 20 + 20 + 20 = 80$$
$$80 + 80 + 80 = 240$$
and you shall continue to multiply.

Let the candles burn down. Place the bill in your purse/wallet, but do not spend it, as you will need to deposit it again on the following Wednesday and withdraw another one on Thursday. Repeat whenever needed.

Sweet Success
If you want it, it's easy.

You will need:

    1 red candle (dress with olive oil)

    1 orange candle (dress with olive oil)

    1 teaspoon of dried basil

    Censer and charcoal

    1 piece of parchment paper

    1 green feather

    1 pinch of nutmeg

    Bottle of blue ink

Light the red and orange candles when the moon is waxing, then light your charcoal and add the dried basil to it. Write the success you seek on the piece of parchment paper by dipping the feather in the blue ink and using it for a pen. Then visualize your success, feel it happening.

Sprinkle the nutmeg on top of your success wish, and say:

> Oh universe divine,
> the one that hears my beating heart,
> The success I need I wish it to be,
> unselfish it is and it will be.

Burn the parchment paper and take the ashes to the highest point in your town such as a hill or a tower, and release them, letting the wind carry your dreams of success and make them real.

Heart, Hurt No More

When the heart hurts, it needs TLC to go on beating.
You will need:

> 1 pink candle (dress with rose oil)
> 1 handful of lavender (an herb)
> 1 rose incense stick
> 1 rose quartz pendant

Light the pink candle, visualize the pain leaving your heart, and say:

> The nights and days will pass,
> So will the pain.

Light the rose incense and hold the rose quartz necklace over the smoke, then sit silently. See the hurt gone, never to return, so you can start fresh and never hurt again. Say:

> Be gone this pain in my aching heart
> I need a fresh start.

Wear the rose quartz necklace and don't take it off until you learn to love the one you should care for the most—your soul.

Friends Again

I want to mend a friendship.

You will need:

> 2 equal pieces of white Play-Doh or white modeling clay
>
> 3 white flowers, white carnations if you can get them
>
> 1 white candle (dress with baby oil)
>
> A picture of you and your friend having fun together
>
> 1 lemon

Light the white candle, visualize what has gone wrong with the friendship, and try to find a way to mend it. Mix the petals of the three white flowers and the seeds of the entire lemon into each piece of Play-Doh. As you knead the Play-Doh pieces, visualize the friendship mending, mixing and blending together once more, then place the picture in front of you and say:

> Leave the past behind
> and the pain in our hearts.
> Friends we will be again
> and this time we will remain.

Make two little people out of the softened Play-Doh. These two figures are you and your friend, and as you make them, feel all the good times you have shared together, and the stupid reason that the friendship fell apart. See that friendship growing once again as you mold the two little figures. Once you're finished, make sure that they are holding hands, and place them on top of the picture.

Let the candle burn down all the way, and wait and see—things will be OK again.

Shields and Swords
Protection my friend needs.

You will need:

    2 blue candles (dress with sesame seed oil)

    A full-length photo of the one you wish to
       protect

    1 square, blue, cotton cloth

    ½ cup of shredded coconut

Light the blue candles, while visualizing the protection

this person needs. Then cover the picture with the blue cloth and sprinkle the shredded coconut on top. As you do this, say:

> Protected you will be
> from those who wish you harm
> in any way.
> Seen be not,
> Heard be not,
> In the eyes and ears of those
> who wish you wrong.

Repeat for about twenty minutes each day for seven days, using the same candles, but with new shredded coconut every day. Keep the picture covered until the end of the seven days.

Bookworm
Hit the books I must.

You will need:

    1 yellow candle (dress with rosemary essential oil)

    1 glass of water

    1 bunch of grapes (not seedless)

When you are ready to hit the books to study, light the yellow candle in your study area, then fill a glass with water, place it next to the candle, and say:

> As clear as this water is, my mind will be
> absorbing everything
> I read this eve.

Begin to study. Eat the grapes one by one, and place the pits inside the glass of water.

When you finish for the night, snuff the candle and go outside and empty the glass of water with the pits on the grass in the backyard.

You can do this little ritual every time you study, and you can use the candle as many times as you like— just get another one when the first one runs out.

Hassle Me No More
Stop being teased.

You will need:

    1 red candle (dress with almond oil)

    1 cup of white sugar

    1 teaspoon of cinnamon

    2 cinnamon sticks

    1 piece of blue paper

Light the red candle on a Tuesday night when the moon is waning.

Write the names of the ones who are causing your stress, and bury their names deep within the sugar.

Sprinkle the cinnamon on top of the sugar, and make an X on top of the cup with the two cinnamon sticks, then say:

> Hassle me no more at school
> or at the corner shops,
> Nice as pie you will be
> to me from now on,
> so be kind if you please.

This will stop the people hassling you and keep them out of your sight.

≈

Keep It to Yourself
Stop the one who talks too much
about the things that hurt others.

You will need:

- 1 glass of water
- 1 piece of parchment paper
- 7 peppercorns
- 1 teaspoon of blue food coloring

On the piece of parchment paper, write the name of the person who is spreading all the harmful gossip. Put the name in the glass of water, then add the seven peppercorns and the blue food coloring.

Stir it all together and, as you do, visualize this person

keeping quiet about the things that are none of her/his business. Imagine this person staying away from the people that she/he likes to attack with harmful gossip, and say:

> Keep away gossip,
> from the one
> who feeds it.

Put the glass of water in the freezer and leave it there for as long as necessary. Take it out if the gossip stops, and if it starts up again, do the same thing all over.

Sourpuss

Help the one who carries anger inside.

You will need:

- 1 lemon
- 1 blue ribbon
- 1 cup of brown sugar
- 1 teaspoon of honey
- 1 piece of parchment paper

Cut off the top of the lemon, then gut it with a spoon. On the parchment paper, write the name of your friend who has been angry. Insert the name inside the lemon and fill the lemon with the brown sugar and honey. Tie the blue ribbon around it to keep it closed, and as you do this say:

> No anger should ever
> come your way again,
> Sour you were and sweet you will remain,
> For the good of all our friends.

Keep the lemon in moonlight for three nights, then keep it safe in a shady place until your friend is sweet once again.

Finders Keepers
Go shopping for friends.

You will need:

- 1 red jasper crystal
- 1 sodalite crystal
- 1 citrine crystal
- 1 malachite
- 1 small purse
- 1 orange

Take the four crystals out into the night on a Wednesday, just before or during a full moon.

Place the four stones on the ground, with the red jasper crystal, which represents the fire element, to the south; the malachite, which represents the earth element, to the north; the citrine, which represents the air element, to the east; and last the sodalite, which represents the water element, to the west.

Place the orange in the middle, and as you do this, visualize the friend you seek and say:

> Elements hear me say
> and help me find
> new true friends.
> Search the east and west,
> Then north and south
> For as long as it takes.

Then eat the orange and pick seeds out of it. Place the seeds inside the purse, together with all the crystals.

Keep this purse with you at all times. After this night, it will always shop around for friends for you and will try to keep them for always.

A Helping Hand
I will no longer be sick.

You will need:

1 pin
1 acorn with cap on
1 blue ribbon

On a Sunday, write your health wish with the pin on top of the acorn, then wrap the entire acorn with the blue ribbon. Find an oak tree, place your bundle at its feet, and say:

> Oh mighty oak,
> I need your strength.
> To help me get well,
> May I hang the acorn from your branches,
> For only three days?

Await a response from the mighty oak—you will know it's OK if a breeze comes your way. When you pick up the acorn after the three days, say:

> Thank you, mighty oak,
> Your strength was all I needed
> to stay healthy and well.

Keep the acorn close to your chest at all times and feel the strength you need to stay healthy and well.

Evil Go Away
Get rid of a hex.

You will need:

1 egg
2 blue candles (dress with almond oil)
1 black candle (dress with olive oil)
1 regular barbeque charcoal
1 pinch of dried angelica
1 pinch of dried damiana
1 charcoal block for your censer

Crack an egg open and keep the shell. Leave it outside for a few days until it is hard and dry enough for you to crush it and make dust out of the shell.

On a Tuesday when the moon is waning, light the two blue candles and use the regular charcoal to draw an imaginary pentagram (five-pointed star) on your altar, to protect you from the evil that is lurking around.

Burn the dried angelica and damiana herbs together on your censer, then anoint your forehead and chest with the eggshell powder. As you do this, say:

> Evil, you shall no longer exist,
> Human or spirit,
> you will terminate this eve,
> Leave this sacred site, my body, and my life.

Light the black candle and make a circle around it with eggshell powder. Then say with strength:

> Stay away and be gone for the good of all.

Snuff the black candle with your fingers and quickly break it in half. Go into the night and leave the black candle where evil resides, and never will you see the face of evil again.

≋

I Can Do This

Everyone can use some extra courage.

You will need:

    1 small brown glass bottle that will hold ¼ cup

    4 teaspoons of almond oil

    1 red, square, cotton cloth

    5 fresh basil leaves

    1 pinch of thyme

Pour the almond oil in the brown bottle and, as you do this, visualize having the inner strength to face anything that comes your way. Add the basil leaves and the dried thyme.

Wrap the red cloth around the bottle, then leave it out in the sun for five hours. Bring it inside the house and leave it in a warm place that gets plenty of sunshine for three days.

Every time courage is needed, just anoint yourself at the back of the neck. The older the mixture gets, the stronger the courage you will have.

≋

Don't Take What Is Not Yours
Stop theft.

You will need:

    3 old keys

    1 handful of caraway seeds

    1 tiger's-eye crystal

    1 black drawstring bag

Keep the caraway seeds, the tiger's-eye crystal, and the three keys in the black drawstring bag.

Keep this in your bookbag at all times. Every day, hold the drawstring bag and say:

> Stay away from what is not yours,
> You thieving teens.

This will stop the ones who like to dig in other people's bags.

Warm and Cozy
Is a friend in need of TLC?

You will need:

    1 blue candle (dress with baby oil)

    1 plush teddy bear

    ½ cup of lavender

    1 blue ribbon

    1 white candle (dress with baby oil)

1 small toy pillow

1 red heart-shaped button

Purchase a teddy bear and make a small opening where the teddy's heart should be, then insert as much of the lavender as you can. Sew up the opening and attach the heart button over your stitches. Light the blue candle while you say:

> Heart be filled with joy,
> Let the pain be gone,
> Warm you will feel,
> Leaving behind the pain so real.

Tie the red ribbon around the neck of the teddy bear in a bow, then gently place his head on the tiny pillow and say:

> Sweet dreams, sweet bear,
> Keep safe and warm the one
> that needs it the most,
> Bring sunshine and hope
> to a very unhappy soul.

Leave the teddy bear alone for one day, then give it as a present to the one who is in need of some TLC, and warm and cosy she or he will feel.

≋

Addiction

Help someone with an addiction,
or help yourself to be free from the chains.

You will need:

    7 red candles (dress with olive oil)

    1 black cloth

    Some of whatever you're addicted to (for
        example, a cigarette)

    1 yard of black ribbon

    1 candle of your astral color (or the addicted
        person's astral color)

Light two of the red candles on a Tuesday night when
the moon is waning. As you do this, visualize what
life was like before the addiction took over. In the
middle of the candles, place the addictive substance
you wish to get rid of. If you are doing this for a friend,
just write down the addiction on a piece of paper.

    Wrap the addictive item or paper with the black
cloth and tie it with the black ribbon. If it's for you,
hold it in your hands and say:

> Never to be seen or used ever again,
> I know I can leave it behind, and I will.

For a friend or family member, say:

> Never to be seen or used ever again,
> I know you can do it

> and leave it behind you shall,
> I'm sending you strength
> to fight the addiction off,
> And please get some needed help.

Place it gently back on top of the table and then light the astral color candle, while visualizing your world, or someone else's, free of this addiction's control. Light the remainder of the red candles, making a circle of flame around your black little parcel, and visualize the pain others are going through because of this addiction, as well as all the harm you are doing to your own soul, which is unhappy and filled with remorse.

Let all the candles burn for a few minutes, and snuff them once you finish. Repeat this the next night at the same time, and every night after that for seven nights.

Note to readers: Please remember that this spell is only a guide to give you the strength needed to overcome an addiction. It does not replace professional help or counseling. Please seek help from friends, family members, your school, or your general practitioner, or look for sites on the Internet on substance abuse. Your body is a temple you have been given to cherish and look after in this lifetime. Take good care of it.

A Spell to Go, Please!

☆ Index of Spells ☆

Spells and Rituals: The Adventure Begins

About the Author

Ileana Abrev has been practicing witchcraft for over ten years. She is also a natural energies consultant and spiritual advisor, guiding her clients in the art of using herbs, crystals, and color to send positive visualizations to the universe for spiritual and personal growth. She also conducts a monthly Magic and Spiritual Workshop to help beginners learn more about this realm, and she is the author of *White Spells*. Ileana loves spending time with her teenaged daughter in their native Australia.